Can we tell you ?...

Dayvaughn Jerome Mays/
Guston Alexander Owens, Jr.

iUniverse, Inc.
New York   Bloomington

Can we tell you ?...

iUniverse books may be ordered through booksellers or by contacting:

iUniverse
1663 Liberty Drive
Bloomington, IN 47403
www.iuniverse.com
1-800-Authors (1-800-288-4677)

ISBN: 978-1-4401-0798-6 (pbk)
ISBN: 978-1-4401-0799-3 (ebk)

Printed in the United States of America

iUniverse rev. date: 3/27/2009

Mission Statement:

As poets we aspire to reach higher by living life through our passion for writing, providing therapy, entertainment, and joy for all readers. Also becoming that voice for those, who, for various reasons, are unable to express openly how they feel. The healing and closure can and will be heard through our writing, we hope to reach many. As we have been inspired to write by life's lessons, our intent is to be that motivation which will allow the hesitant to speak and stand up without compromise, but do it with respect, dignity, and a certain level of sensitivity to others, we will be understood. As you get to know us, very quickly, you will conclude we are very similar to you, a visual tape recorder constantly recording, absorbing, internalizing, and forming opinions to be, in most cases, stored away and never again retrieved. To that end, we're driven to rewind and press play so the masses can unite and realize, as human beings, we all are very much the same, though cosmetically, economically, and socially different. Together we can meet at your favorite get away location, stand on common ground, and communicate without inhibitions. After our encounter, we will forever be connected through words of reception, and if we choose to, continue to grace one another with strength and gifting, as we pass what we've shared to those in our paths. If for some reason we only measure our similarities and growth on one occasion, may your journey be blessed and patterned in love, giving, peace, and total fulfillment. For those that are engaged, let's ride the radiant rainbow while the showers precipitate the blossoming of the newly planted seed we all seek for positive and inspirational change. We sincerely thank you for your time.

1. My Season

If you know The Word or even if you don't, for everything there's a
    reason
Things don't just happen, hence a time and a season
I'm inclined to rewind and recollect on the past waiting for a sign
To unwind my thoughts and experiences, some carnal some in nature
    divine
Many deep, mentally penetrating breaking barriers crossing the
    comfort line
I'm ready to shoot, not from the barrel of a gun but from the barrel of
    my mind
God set the alarm clock, recently it sounded off so now it's time
Connecting directly with the reader with each line
Whether graphic and intimidating based on reality, or fantasy like
    subtle and sublime
On this wonderful journey I hope to explore territory untapped new
    discoveries and more
Stay true to my roots, continue to be me right down to the core
Without compromise unsure through my travels what's in store
But that's the allure, unknown potential reaching for the highest score
I give you me from my heart to yours so you adore
Together our intellect connects we bond mentally as one we soar
Flying as high as we choose, the wind beneath our wings full of good
    spirits we sing
Reminiscing on former things, at times tugging on the high level of
    sensitivity strings
Our emotional ride together back and forth swings
With mutual support we track and report as we engage
Me and you center stage, in unison on the same page

It's been a long time coming I've been seeking, always running but
      past tense
It wasn't making sense, now running I've hurdled the capturing
      closed fence
Haven't looked back since, I'm taking all who are ready, seeing my
      180 now convinced
Let's roll I'm ready for all the right reasons
God said it's time, my light shines, it's My Season

Guston Alexander Owens, Jr.

2. Fate

You strive to survive and just stay alive
And right now you have time it's never too late
But don't tempt your fate because soon He won't wait
So roll with the The Lord because eternal life is at stake
There are two types of angels so please don't mistake
The one that does love you for the other one which hates
Be saved and blessed eternal don't contemplate or debate
Repent right now or the Lord will forsake
It's all in your hands it's up to you to dictate
Your own will is your guide as your actions relate
You want love and peace not torture and hate
So crucify your flesh as on the Lord you await
Man is appointed to live once so where will you awake
Will it be Heaven or hell as your spot you will take
You can be phony if you choose but the Lord you can't fake
Straddling the fence He won't open the gate
To eternity and bliss the ride you will not make
Tomorrow is not promised so today make it great
If you don't care don't despair there you have it your Fate

Guston Alexander Owens, Jr.

3. Contradiction

Is it possible to cooperate and disagree
Can I be standing right here and at the same time flee
Appear to be afloat under water as I sink
Have absolutely nothing on my mind, at the same time think
Take something back and simultaneously give
Be terribly afraid to die vexed, meanwhile fearing to live
Purposely move forward and accidentally regress
Completely shut out ignored, but still manage to impress
Absolutely sincere without my words matching my heart
At the finish line invigorated but barely enough energy to start
Victorious falling in the face of defeat
Or a loser erect still standing on my feet
Carefully cautious yet ticking about to explode
Or heedless living dangerously in complete control
Having faith doubting The Word not telling my story
Totally faithless following God giving Him all the glory
Are these things possible, yes, well no it depends on your position
Every step we take, every move we make, ponders Contradiction.

Guston Alexander Owens, Jr.

4. Paradise

Is it my current location or my preferred destination
Is it physical or in the inner depths of my heart and soul where I seek
    resignation
From the trials and tribulations life deals with no reservations
Constant complications and ailments, deceit, impalement
My pain I internalize, my goal to realize, a short time I compromise
Keeping focused my eyes on the ultimate prize
Bliss, heaven, and extreme delight
I await on the Lord, He's coming but like a thief in the night
My plight, stay on course continue the fight
Sometimes wrong but I try to do right
In spite on my flight I'm doing good
Tripped up sought out by temptation, every now and then out comes
    the hood
Convicted, glory restricted, my flesh conflicted, it felt right at the time
Vexed, I want to call someone but I'm short one dime
For my crime doing time, mentally it's always on my mind
Repent prayed to God for forgiveness I'm just waiting for a sign
Divine in nature to help me escape the guilt and the shame
The Word says I'm forgiven but I still call His name
Finally realizing my stay here I will forever be enticed
No fear, have faith, as I transition to eternal Paradise

Guston Alexander Owens, Jr.

5. Grounded

Is this so because I'm level headed and have a strong foundation
Or levitating sky high, arrogant knocked down by motivation
Of those around me surrounding me invading my territory
Attempting to steal what's mine, my success and my glory
Have I struck out grounded out as I'm up to bat at the plate
Did I make a wrong move, take a bad turn, is this my mistake
Was it flamboyancy, self righteousness, give me mine I deserve it
Or in the same game swinging fast, the pitcher pitched and he curved it
Swing and miss, swung hard, as before your feet were planted
What you have, what you are, was this all taken for granted.
If you assumed this was bottomless and forever this would last
Take a look where you are not always there, you had a past
A past where humbleness, short lived however apparent
It was in you, it's in us all at birth, it's inherent
As a child of God we're born humble as I have aforementioned
Keeping it, staying grounded, unfortunately is not the masses intention
Swayed by success and only one way to get it, unaffected by contention
Keep that frame of mind, stepping on others but, I forgot to mention
You'll fall with reverberations that will be felt and resounded
This will be and shall be the ideal way, you will find yourself
    Grounded

Guston Alexander Owens, Jr.

6. Life's Elements

Life's Elements, we pursue with vigor, and great elegance
Anything else in your path is irrelevant, what you up against
Shame, arrogance, is it your past, future, or current present tense
Are you on the fence, or the defense captured defenseless
Life's quarrels are sometimes grueling and relentless
So now you get this but it's eventless, no glory in it so you're listless
Caught shiftless so to cause a lift you pump, pump your fist
Your existence is more than what's around your neck or on your wrist
If you're conscious you got this, you can rock this but can't mock this
It's original appeals to your conscious mind not the subliminal
Giving God the glory is the pinnacle, living life to the fullest not
    being cynical
Grab hold and pull make everyday adventurous not slow and dull
Tomorrow is never promised, so don't let it lull
Corral the horns but don't take the constant bull, away from it,
    yourself you pull
Positivity and pursuant of goals keeps your basket full
Be of good courage search your heart for purity, on your journey
    don't get discouraged
It'll emerge once you feel it, full of vitality forward you'll surge
Soon on the congested highway of life, opportunity and preparedness
    will merge
Listen when the cat purrs, that's an agreement a concur
Contentment as he licks his fur, bliss found even if just for a moment
It's rejuvenating restores energy to every component
Don't get lost in the worn down shuffle
Or your very being will go unseen, unheard, you'll be muffled
Forgotten, left out right where you're standing

No more support, every group you're part of because of you is now
    disbanding
This happens quickly with little or no understanding
So turn on your heart and learn to give, that's why we live
Pure enjoyment when you pick someone else up
You'll be fulfilled and thrilled as someone else fills your cup
Its reciprocation and good will that keeps us benevolent
Love is and always will be the greatest of Life's Elements

Guston Alexander Owens, Jr.

7. Life and Death

God gave us life so it is essential
Death comes after life which makes it eventual
Life plus Death reveals a common denominator
In us all, where we spend eternity will be an indicator
Of what we did while we lived passing between the two
Who we worshipped, who we followed is how we make it through
The gates of heaven or the depths of hell, what story will you tell
To get to the Father is through the Son the rest is old failed tales
Believe what you want it is your own will, but with caution please proceed
If you're believing to pass to eternal bliss, it's Jesus that you need
For it is written a man is appointed to live but once and then to die
Will you be cast to eternal damnation, or catapulted to an infinite high
It's an account of your life is what you will be giving
You can't run, you cant hide, it'll be playing how you were living
So believers repent and one thing is for sure, your soul will not be left
Is it heaven or hell, your life will tell, once you've passed through Life
    and Death

Guston Alexander Owens, Jr.

8. Cast Your Vote

I begin to choke as I cast my vote
Unsure who to cast for as the masses provoke
My decision, with intense intimidation
Swaying me with emphatic reasons regarding who's qualified to run
    the nation
I pause with hesitation, thoughts of corruption my reservation
Life as we know it dies, ending in cremation
Numb to disaster, insensitive, no sensation
Not even a burial, no celebration
Stored in an urn after incineration
Being burned as the hard lesson learned, that we have no say so in the
    delegation
In turn we elect the lesser of two evils
One white, one black, two men but not equals
As the race card is pulled
Unnecessary however a necessity
So please don't be fooled
By the seemingly sincere passion
As they placate with great fashion
Lying through their teeth like the devil he's gnashin'
While devouring our souls, leading us we're sold
Simply because we chose by the process of elimination
Slowly we decay, painfully by degradation
Based on the leadership of one of the two
If I had a say so it would be me, or I'd pick you
Since that's not possible, I'll leave you on this note
Here's a thought, there's the trash, I cast my vote

Guston Alexander Owens, Jr.

9. Obama for America

Obama for America, the possibility causing mass hysteria
Will he mend, or continue to bend the nation's quality of life in every
    area
United we stand individually we fall
We've been divided, dialing for answers, who will step up to take the
    call
Will it be a first or is it rehearsed
Looked at as a blessing could very well be a curse
Is America prepared for a minority in authority, will we be the
    priority
Or will the economic benefits continue to flow through the majority
The man himself looks polished almost flawless, has gained notoriety
Look closely, pay attention there's evidence of impiety
Perhaps we should elect Dr. Jeckyll and Mr. Hyde
Two unstable leaders running the country side by side
That stated think about it is there really a difference
The President is both Jeckyll and Hyde, delivering America quite a
    hindrance
Today he's for this against that what the heck
Tomorrow he's for that against this spewing interchangeably out of
    both sides of his neck
Speech by speech these actions get older, as our very being smolders
Aimlessly we wander into an ultimate direction, as bitterly approaches
    the election
Our sanity and quality of life seeks demonstrated correction
Our leader so poetic could he perhaps be the anomaly
Words spoken, carefully chosen delivered emphatically yet calmly

Our decision driven by desperation as death for America is imminent
One by one we pass slowly, our own blood we die in it
Lackluster in movement no progress, tomorrow we hope we can say
Obama for America, otherwise it's demise just like yesterday

Guston Alexander Owens, Jr.

10. Republicrat

The two headed monster is upon us mesmerizing with his scripted
    grammar
Smooth, exciting, tantalizing, delivering without a stutter or stammer
We convoke at the Republicrats beckoned call
The economy continues to rapidly fall
Eluding to change empowering the people
Death to America continues as the sequel
Because of our arrogance 9-11 was just the beginning
We're losing and losing fast, but led to believe we're winning
More of this gushing out of his orifice
The very sound is torturous, as he propitiates to make amends
It's all caught on tape as his actions pretend
Very important his day is booked, check the itinerary
Who's involved, what's the goal at the end of the day, who's the
    beneficiary
Is it all a hoax to receive the majority vote
America's stuck in the middle as we're forced to choke
On a decision that must be made with pain
One by one slowly we vote as the country's being slain
Unfortunately don't lose the perspective, the objective, be selective
Who's the least deceptive, as to one we must be receptive
In the end most will lose as the winner we choose
Will continue to beat us down an everlasting bruise
If we don't vote it's considered a selfish act
Here you go, there's my vote, and the winner is The Republicrat

Guston Alexander Owens, Jr.

11. Greed's Plight

The world has changed for good
Not for the good, so don't get it misunderstood
The drudgery of everyday survival is widespread
Not just the poor with no money, even the rich with no worries end
     it, found dead
Tricked for life believing money makes them secure
That focus neglects the realities, for there are more important things
     to endure
Sure money makes the world go round
But can also place you quickly six feet underground
You have it they want it
Like you they'll do anything to get it and flaunt it
Compromise integrity step on those in our tunnel vision path
Clean up the mess never confess, no participation in the blood bath
Life as a whole becomes meaningless and cold
Nothing matters as every fiber of our being is sold
To be materialistically enhanced here's the chance to advance
To the top of the socioeconomic ladder
How'd you get there, no one asks, it doesn't really matter
You made it they didn't you were at the top of your game
Stressed and strained, morals shaken but no feelings of shame
Isn't that how everyone goes out to get it
Guilt suppressed conditioned to hide it, but your soul will never
     forget it
Though unseen there's a void inside that cries out to be filled
You live life status quo as you're slowly being killed
By your obsession turned depression
x-ray negative, your sickness no detection

Visit after visit bill after bill
Finally diagnosed as depression you're mentally ill
Prescribed a pill, what's the deal, doctor said it would help who am I
    to appeal
It's real unable to accept change you rebel
Day by day your life's torturous a living hell
Stock market crashes you lose money by the masses
Still loaded your mind and reality clashes
Blinded by your need to feed your greed you no longer feel you can
    succeed
Your soul pleads but your heart bleeds
You don't know the Lord so your whole life you pretended
Death speaks to you in a whisper there's the gun, you end it

                                    Guston Alexander Owens, Jr.

12. The Deficit

The Deficit, yeah it trickles down
The government inks the dough but in my bank account it's scarcely
    found
Trillions upon trillions they say we're in the hole
Somehow the rich get richer, the poor get poorer as we sell our soul
To obtain the almighty dollar forget about health
Rob and steal even kill to attain the elusive wealth
Politicians always mention, their intention is to strengthen
While our bank accounts are overdrawn theirs continue to lengthen
To amounts too massive for one account so they diversify
Stockbrokers moving money, inside trading no need to ask why
No questions asked as the decimals move to the right speedily
Balances checked frequently, consuming wants abundantly and
    greedily
The stimulus for us was temporary and false hope
We waited anticipated that we might now be able to cope
Get ahead, stay ahead presented a new beginning
Attempt to catch up on our bills, still losing no winning
Stimulate the struggling economy who are they kidding
Bill collectors, the grocery store stood in line as they were bidding
For a portion similar to extortion with their bullying psychological
    tactics
We're still failing like a fish flailing, it's apparent and the fact is
Faced with a recession, families filled with depression they strategize a
    bailout
A corporate restructure, a reduction, these overpaid execs need to get
    the hell out
No more yachts, no more Bentleys, butlers or maids

No more trips company paid being served in the shade
By the frontline in the sunshine not a stress worry or care
Wardrobe delivered dry cleaned, only dilemma, what to wear
New bailout plan hit them where they hit us then they'll quit
No more control, no more lavishness, now that's The Deficit

Guston Alexander Owens, Jr.

13. The Dream

As it's given by the non winner the speech of concession
Half of America is stuck in depression
There's winds of change as he concedes
It's agreed it's a need but has our mind been freed
Will this close the book for this life long pursuit for change
Or is it similar to a cell phone with no service out of range
Isn't that strange, all the losses few gains
As we wake up tomorrow with new vigor catapulting from the former
    strains
Has our stock been invested in and quickly risen
Or lost in reality, many black men still heading to prison
Blacks feeling as if the ultimate has been achieved
It's believed somehow we're no longer grieved
Deceived perhaps, but we can keep hope alive
Check out our stride as we work harder and strive
To no longer be secondary as one man has a people thinking
    legendary
A people for life labeled complacent and sedentary
Will we rise to the unprecedented occasion
Or maintain bullishly in the former, still apparent persuasion
Second and in some cases third place in the Race
Can we collaborate, coexist, promote change with the irremovable
    smirk on our face
A bad taste and disgrace as we chase in slow haste
Success like our counterparts futility at its peak, much time we must waste
A jolt of confidence steroidal in its affect
No more back of the bus mentality or credit rejects
Much respect, as the privileged are somewhat astounded

Is this a new breed of black, superior whitey is confounded
Dumbfounded, in retrospect to a former place and time
When our mind was confined, many thoughts of committing crimes
Sublimed in our conduct we're now deemed worthy
Positive is our mannerism, no need to be scurvy
As a whole we're not bitter, no longer quitters
Welfare a thing of the past black mothers seeking baby sitters
Men of color competitors, no longer predators seeking now to advance
On the job working hard realizing a never before chance
Less sagging and bragging, collar popping, brand name tagging
More reading mind feeding vocabulary growing
Educated well related confidence and abilities showing
Pushing forward no looking back with a full head of steam
Is this reality or a fantasy as tomorrow we awake hostile, from The Dream

Guston Alexander Owens, Jr.

14. American Flag

The stars and stripes symbolize the groans and gripes wrongs and rights
We attempt to embrace but continue to resist and fight
Our enemies despise plotting and strategizing to make us realize
Their goal is our demise, America sees freedom in the red white and blue
The rivals want us dead in spite for what we do
To them the stars reflect an explosion, corruption, erosion
The stripes the end result our country flat lined, that's their notion
Constantly in motion conjuring up the deadly potion
Feeding us while we're carefree and watch us as we die in slow
    commotion
Painful, agonizing we hear with a deaf ear the whistling train, death
    by locomotion
Tied to the tracks unable to escape the wrath
America's pride and arrogance as we stumble into that fateful path
Struggle, deceit, and hate we all participate in the blood bath
Constantly pointing the finger at whose to blame the enemy sits back
    and laughs
Charts and graphs at hand is the task to regroup
Counter attack against the wall is our backs
Dominance no longer real preparedness we lack distract is the
    ultimate strategy
Make us feel safe with peaceful diversions amidst all the grief death
    and tragedy
It's sad to see our troops dying in groups
Perilous times will never end the losses none of which we can recoup
It's not enough but to the front line a moment of silence and a salute
Families left slighted depression and hard times ignited

Babies growing up never knowing that integral part, the evils
  delighted
Pictures of moms and dads their only existence it's hard to be excited
No memory of voice bonding or loving touch
You know in your heart it's there, the only helpful mental crutch
As such, left empty not seeking sympathy
Everyone has their own demons to deal with no time for empathy
America, the land of the free how can that be
Maybe physically, captured mentally your mind attempts to flee
Bitterly pledging allegiance choking as we all gag
Decimated, one by one by the targeted American Flag

Guston Alexander Owens, Jr.

15. We Salute

This oration is a needed dedication to the men and women of our
    nation
Who without hesitation, serve and die for the masses because of
    others disagreements and unresolved complications, after a
    short time in the trenches some need medication
Silent and dead inside but trained in constant communication, the
    duration
Infinite in calculation, mind forever a projector replayed frustration
Terror, sleeplessness mental degradation slowly left out of the main
    stream disassociation
Modification of benefits doctors care given but with costly limitations
Take 6 of these daily won't cure but for a short time in between
    relieve your situation
Now dependent hooked, anxiety at peaked levels when closed is the
    pharmacy location
Desperate, living in poverty without a real occupation
The government you served sends a menial check monthly to show
    appreciation
Those 6 pills prescribed no longer help no sensation
In need of something to take away the pain, arm now filled with
    striations
Dope man delivers now you're a slave on a plantation
To the drug you require twice a day to shoot up that's the application
In desperation, money short robbing and stealing your new vocation

Anyone's a target open market penetration
Jailed for life, no jury sentenced without deliberation
The reward from the country you served faithfully a long vacation
Seems like yesterday gung ho you were the recruit
Thank you once again from America, to you We Salute

Guston Alexander Owens, Jr.

16. Love Is

Love is not a flower prepared to bloom
Love is holding on standing strong when all about is gloom
Love is unconditional and complete sincerity
True unchangeable with no need for clarity
Love is a solid rock to stand on when things are unstable
A boost, a cheer, a shoulder to cry on until once again you're able
Love is compromise to the extent of one hundred percent
Pushing self aside never having to resent
Love is passionate, giving not intending to take
Forgiving, always apparent it shines in lieu of any mistake
Love is shelter an umbrella when it's pouring rain
A dose of sunshine therapy in time to ease the pain
Love is held near and dear as a blanket of security
Comfort, reassurance as the outcome reaches obscurity
Love is a bear hug as bad news is revealed
Staying in your corner as you profess your innocence when the
        verdicts appealed
Love is stepping in to help in a bleak situation
Listening without opinion while someone vents their frustration
Love is keeping your word showing up to help as planned
Even if at the last minute something comes up, still there for your
        fellow man
Love is giving without expecting anything in return
Constant and continuous even when it results in being burned
God is love and He is the very meaning of how to give
He died for all of humanity, the ultimate of what Love Is

Guston Alexander Owens, Jr.

17. Distance Between Brothers

Time the only distance between two brothers
Many commonalities shared the greatest one a strong mother
Who went home to be with the Lord many years ago
Her strength, lovingness, and gentleness in us still shows
Fatherless men grew up as men the best they could
Persevered through struggles and discouragement like real men would
No excuses both willing to pay the price for their mistakes
Keeping it real is our motto no time to be fake
Born leaders no real enemies typically admired by all
Always willing to help out others sometimes our downfall
In many situations taken advantaged of
We seek our strength and courage from our omnipotent God above
We know Jesus loves us unconditionally
We seek Him in spirit for guidance in our heart and mentally
The world is a tough place full of hard times and despair
Engulfed with hate and deceit for others most don't care
God has us both where we are for our own protection
Though our current location might not be our selection
Correction is what we ultimately seek
Whether behind concrete walls or stepping free on the streets
Never complete, our mind at times is our biggest obstacle
Controlling our actions we suffer but make it even through the
     impossible
With the Lord in our lives we cannot lose
We're forgiven when we repent no matter the path we choose
In caution we take heed as we proceed, God will provide for our every
     need
In the end we succeed heaven bound finally freed

Brothers in Christ and creation, children of the Almighty our greatest
    relation
In our hearts we're close near and dear like our mother
Again, time is the only real Distance Between Brothers

                               Guston Alexander Owens, Jr.

18. Poetry in Motion

Poetry in motion what is it, I can relate what it means to me
It's serenity, therapeutic, an escape from reality
A mental massage a beautiful corsage enlightening and feeling
    carefree
A welcoming sigh, an emotional high, dismissing life's harsh realities
A fantasy real eye candy unmatched appeal, endless bliss as deep as
    the sea
Smooth terrain, drops of sweet rain, dripping slowly on your favorite
    bag of tea
Tasty wine, stunning rays of sunshine captivating fall leaves on a tree
A peaceful drive, a wave less boat ride, a picturesque vision of eternity
Tall blades of green grass, velvety white beach sand, a colorful
    rainbow as far as the eye can see
The smell of alluring perfume, a heightening ride in an air balloon, a
    casual walk in the cool evening breeze
So if you see me and I seem distant, please don't be resistant, Poetry
    in Motion is where I'll be

Guston Alexander Owens, Jr.

19. Thanksgiving

A mental time also filled with lots of turkey and dressing
Recollection and resurrection of past struggles turned to blessings
Emotions lifted, past and current experiences sifted
One by one, overwhelmed understanding how you're so gifted
By God's grace and His everlasting merciful love
Mistakes forgiven, He allows you to keep on living as you seek heaven above
Embattled mindset battling self, flesh feeling much lack
You watch as others seem to be over pouring with gain continuing to stack
You attack, the one in the mirror at you looking back
Reckless thoughts of aggression you attempt to pick up the slack
By any means necessary, out of character you begin to act
Feeling blessed spiritually, but carnally to everything is how you react
In fact, usually respectful your metamorphosis is without tact
Your whole life is out of whack
Thrown off by your actions you're out of balance
Searching deeply asking God for forgiveness, seeking guidance
    towards your talents
Granted still slanted driven to fly straight the seed for cure has been
    planted
The masses need reaching through your words you begin teaching
Anointed by The Lord no time to deal with impeaching
Still not perfect His Word is delivered because of Him with
    perfection
His prophecy will be fulfilled it is written, without exception
Your protection is your decision one selection
The detection, how you love others from the heart
Spreading your testimony held up strong as you impart
The good Lord's might love and omnipotence

Helping those around you like you who are at times straddling the fence
Your defense, my flesh is weak give it to Jesus doesn't matter the
    expense
Costly it will be without repentance at times the course you take
    makes little sense
In it God will be glorified whether past, future, or present tense
Finally convinced crying out to Him you realize you're defeated
Outnumbered by evil God intervenes as the enemy has now retreated
The Lord is now the driver of your life buckled in now a passenger
    properly seated
So much to be thankful for it's for The Lord you keep on living
Glory be to God forever we give Thee Thanksgiving

Guston Alexander Owens, Jr.

20. This Woman's Worth

Priceless despite it's just a word
Showing her she is resoundingly heard
Giving completely without reservations
Doing it without complaining, consistently, no hesitation
At times she might mention how tired she is
But with love and great care she continues to give
And lives for God first and family second
Don't get in her way she's a force to be reckoned
Wit is uncanny, bodacious and sexy is her fanny
Coveted like total fulfillment and success
She lives to give her man more, never less
Success for her is seeing the man in her life smile
Tirelessly striving to be his everything her efforts worthwhile
Faithful without a second thought or deviation, always reliable
Loving unconditionally, passionately, undeniable
Revering in her position in control at the helm
The encourager, silently, one touch soothes when life overwhelms
The real captain of the ship well equipped never trips
Speaks when necessary knows when to bite her lip
Submits, not grudgingly but lovingly the apparent backbone
Holds everything together with sensitivity, yet stable and strong
Beauty at its peak, effervescent when she speaks
Others seek but can't compete, she's fulfilled totally complete
For her family she'd walk to the ends of the earth
If you didn't know I hope you now understand, This Woman's Worth

Guston Alexander Owens, Jr.

21. Raggedy Man

You see him all the time you know this man
Some nights he's asleep, right next to Raggedy Ann
In the winter his skin is pale in the summer he has a nice tan
Not really that popular, he's his number one fan
Mostly shopping in vacancies and the depths of a garbage can
He lives rent free on the bare streets of this free land
Some despise others lend a kind gesture a helping hand
Here you go my man, some change dropped in his coveted pan
And within a short span he's feeling grand
He just copped, now with a fifth in his hand
Talkative, inhibitions fade with each gulping swallow
He now has a lot to say voice dry, deep, and hollow
Words of wisdom spoken but deemed insignificant, shallow
No one's willing to listen so in his own pity he wallows
He's misunderstood which is not really a surprise
Those around him look down on his very being with a veer and
    scowling eyes
Not for a moment empathizing considering what led to his demise
Confidence and stature from life's beat down daily, reduced in size
His skin dry and peeling, his smell stale he wreaks and by anyone in
    his path despised
Late to bed late to rise he wakes up when he's ready without
    compromise
The occasional harassment from those on patrol as he attempts to rest
Nomadic he's back at it, where you see him is where he lives a floating
    address
No mail delivery some nights are cold he's shivery

Help from the bottled brown bag takes the chill off the moon shines
 it's shimmery
Internally he's warmed pleasant thoughts of his childhood jolts his
 memory
Quietly he pretends to be significant, prominent restoring his identity
Reality quickly takes its place as he swigs his last sip
An empty bottle, a bad taste, a frowned face, cracked lips
Before a real tear falls the sand man intervenes, a deep sleep he into
 now slips
Now dreaming in his favorite place a fantasy land
There he's king and on his own two feet he can proudly stand
Don't judge, inside we all resemble the distant, infamous, Raggedy
 Man

Guston Alexander Owens, Jr.

22. Cold Caller

Really I'm a warm being but my tactics are cold blooded
The sold are somewhat confused, overwhelmed, mind flooded
Equilibrium shaken just bought, but unsure if they understand
Gung ho about more free, to their peers of course they'll recommend
Still unclear something stuck relating to great potential
They agreed I didn't force the transaction completely consensual
Certain concerns went unanswered, you slid through didn't tell them
Impulsive, off balance hit hard your assault damaged their cerebellum
The deal is finally sealed everything important to close you revealed
Anything thought to be a showstopper rightfully concealed
That's every sales persons appeal, simply put, part of the spiel
If you're on my side of the dialogue I'm sure one can relate
I'm paid on accumulated numbers no time to debate
Preying on anyone who'll listen, my charm glistens
Plethoric as I verbalize hitting on all cylinders nothing missing
Hissing like a snake in attack mode slithering
It's crunch time, the close is what I'm delivering
Uncovering needs to feed my greed
I'll sell it to you whether you require it or not, buyers take heed
My compensation is the seed, planted by corporate greed
If minimums aren't met slim chance to succeed
My objection, to sell you what you are to me a hot lead
Attempting to interest you with reason if that fails plead
Can't recede, too much time invested to get your attention
Pushing to hear you commit little regard for retention
Did I mention, someone else will hold you to that accord
You did say yes I believe I pushed the button to record
It's official I'm on to the next call

Waiting to hear the subsequent objection, the next stall
On my way to the end of my day mentally I begin to fall
Finally after nine hours I'm off to rest not for the weak everyday a
     new test
Five days in repetition aggression similar to a pit bull mauler
Step by step, you now understand a day in the life of a Cold Caller

Guston Alexander Owens, Jr.

23. I'm On Their Ear

Listen you hear me revving I'm coming
It's been a long journey a million miles still running
Mentally stunning, the accelerator to the floor I'm gunning
Fast pace not yet seen in the race
Evidence of existence but unseen is my face
Others state my case having sampled a small taste
Eager to help pedal my words to the masses at a rapid pace
You can listen all you need in your capacity is a small space
The place, right where you are a quick sample
Filled with situations, conditions, and life's metaphoric examples
For a moment your mind's trampled
Left in deep thought brain cells crumbling, dismantled
So provokingly scripted it sounds far from the truth
Takes on the possibility it was rehearsed in a booth
Uncouth, I write day and night not to excite
Hopefully to help and make a few wrongs right
To encourage and reunite those desolate relationships and ignite
World peace and love universally, putting God first and His might
My plight, to be heard change your way of thinking as you read every word
Not to shame just put you up on game
If you need to point a finger I'm the one you should blame
No need to know my name you'll know me by my footprints left on
        your brain
It won't change the affect remains the same
It might become exposure but in the end will ease the pain
Suppressing your demons will lead to medication, stress, and strain
Releasing it is not a loss but well being and gain
If you're still listening you're lubricated, glistening

I'm soliciting to spark a light in the dark
Hark, don't lose me together we're in too deep
When I'm finished you'll retire and require a little sleep
What's the code, let me tap into your intellect
Never mind I'm hacking but I mean no disrespect
A heat check, with this I'm as sick as the flu you can gauge
Therapeutic with my jargon healing the sick and quietly calming the
    enraged
You're engaged, focused on me I'm center stage
Massaging you through your injuries you're unleashed from being caged
My expected wage, apply what I mentioned
Passing along your experience hopefully is your intention
Retention will be easy even if I'm not near
Don't fear, if I'm on your mind I'm On Their Ear

                                    Guston Alexander Owens, Jr.

24. Thoughts for Food

My mind is so deep you can fall in it, if you got game post up and
    ball in it
If you need to pause and think you can stop and stall in it
Fighting off demons take your position and brawl in it, we're all in it
Another visual replayed constantly in your mind like a residual
You won't forget like a special occasion, images memorable
Stretched to reach universally but starts with the individual
Gifted to all in its path worthy, it's commendable
If absorbed and applied consistently very dependable
Results new and improved like a good doctor recommendable
Never expendable, my words of wisdom are classy and authentic not plastic
Truth the real deal not stretched like elastic, provokingly laid back or
    drastic
Outcome fantastic never outlasted if passed it's positive, mental,
    beneficial
Very apparent, obvious not unclear and suspenseful
A marathon, stamina built up, an event so it's eventful
You'll learn patience, love, and care and not be so resentful
Confidence again in life making it blissful
With God's help you search within, that's where it begins
Straight forward with your dealings no more time to pretend
You make amends a helping hand to all you offer to lend
In positivity your time is where you desire to spend
Strangers are like friends on your face a permanent grin
It's infectious those in your path reciprocate showing dimples on their
    cheeks and chin
Now a winner, in your presence we all win that's the spin on life you
    chose

Quickly freed from negativity to the top you rose
Doors are open once closed foes now allies very recently, you they
    opposed
The new light in you shines radiantly and it shows as your leadership
    grows
Now an inspiration you inspire helping many around you climb
    higher
To achieve their goals and desires, humbly you take compliments
    you're admired
Fuel for the fire you're only human so you tire
Easily rejuvenated by the love given back you keep on giving without lack
On your journey you're attacked God is with you so He picks up the slack
He keeps you motivated and on track so your life doesn't spiral and
    get out of whack
He's got your back even when you're not in the mood
He's your strength and courage keeps you fit to continue to dish,
    Thoughts for Food

Guston Alexander Owens, Jr.

25. Stuck Slipping

Potential for damage is right here but I don't need it
I'm trying to bulk up in my passion so I feed it
Knowledge the gateway to success so now I read it
Breaking the law is a lost cause, staying away from it is how I beat it
Arrogance slides my way but I check it now it retreated
Torn apart it tips away embarrassed, defeated
The movement is slow accelerator to the floor is how I speed it
Leadership dissipating, stepping up now I lead it
Running from trouble the usual way now it's greeted
Wisdom from others I'm listening now I heed it
Money is low but to live I know I need it
A baker with dough stretched to grow, flour and water massaging I
    knead it
My stories are true fact based so you believe it
Spilling so much my tanks low close to depleted
Strategizing to the top I won't share so selfishly I keep it
Sowing it out is how I get it back that's how I reap it
Damaging others on the low not caught creeping
Being true to myself and others only when sleeping
The slope is slippery now as it steepens
Situations out of hand as the plot deepens
Out of control I lose hold out of my actions the truth is seeping
Can't cope off life's ledge I contemplate leaping
When I'm gone you move on no time for weeping
Under the rug all my dirt, when no one's looking begin sweeping
I said it once it's not worth me repeating
My pen's getting heavy my story I attempt completing
As this chronicle ends and if the flow you're no longer feeling

Check for infringement a thief didn't get caught stealing
You'll know if it's me because I expose and my words are revealing
Sometimes dark and scary but capturing and appealing
Keeps you hooked spiraling and reeling
Your emotional ride is up and down from the floor to the ceiling
Take a deep breath temptation and selfishness will have you tripping
Seek resolution at all costs, or you'll be like the masses Stuck Slipping

Guston Alexander Owens, Jr.

26. The Basement Of The Mind

I'm there it's part of my mentality
You'll find me there in the darkest corners of reality
It's found in me, I'm tied up bound it's confounding me
Too much evil and degradation surrounding me
I'm kin to the crooked, one loose strap from a straight jacket
Too much on my plate to juggle, peace of mind I lack it
Problem after problem I can't face, in a pile I stack it
If I had a steady wall around me the infamous pile I'd rack it
Better structure, mind somewhat clearer if it was I'd attack it
Maybe later but for now I seek relaxation, stumbling and staggering
     to isolation
So tomorrow I'll be ready to battle full of rejuvenation
So high from feeling low brain flutters with hallucination
Speech stutters in communication, all alone I'm shy forming new
     relations
Not a quitter so I promised myself I'd continue to fight with extreme
     dedication
Burdened to coexist, my interaction is done painfully out of hesitation
Comprehension level on course for fast deterioration
I see things that are different as the same can't distinguish falling into
     amalgamation
Everything once fun, to it now I'm numb, little if any sensation
Self counseling futile can't hear myself think, so no penetration
Desperately I race in haste to cover up my misery without a trace
So everyday I apply mental make-up to my face
A reckless façade to conceal the disgrace, what a waste
Every endeavor is dull, robotic without taste
I need help but no one's there, quietly I plead my case

I feel better down here at the basement level
The world caused me to dwell here life's a shovel
Real soon I'll be close enough to shake hands with the devil
Now a psyched out rebel, too much despair up there beyond repair
I'm comfortable with every step to a lowering level down these stairs
If I don't show up tomorrow who will care
No one ever really acknowledged me, rarely shared
Their phony placating actions toward me can now be spared
There it is my best friend, the reclined chair
On my way to it I took my last step I have resigned
Now lost but if you look hard enough and have the key you will find
There's a multitude of us missing trapped, in The Basement of the
    Mind

                              Guston Alexander Owens, Jr.

1. IN THE MOOD

I was in the mood
To expose my life
So, here is me in the nude
My views, my blues, my attitude
My gratitude
To those who give me conversation
Observation, suggesting alterations
Not that I have Solomon's wisdom
But I search and I'm versed in the traditions and izms
I look you in the eyes and listen
To friends and strangers stories
Some slow to talk
Others begging explore me
I share mine and I find it relaxing
To give a piece of me
Whether a big piece or a fraction
Getting things said
Before people start asking
Sometimes a bad reaction
Point of views end up clashing
Contractions happen
When you are letting out dirt
Best to release hurt
Before you sleep in the Earth
I'm spiritual, I'm for spiritual Israel
I sin, but it isn't sin
If it doesn't fall, within the 10
I don't judge, I have issues

I need help at times
If you can't feel the whole book
Maybe you felt one line
Thanks for your time
Your support, your purchase
Poetry can be a service
Open minds give purpose
Politics or religion
Relationships, decisions
The fantastic encounters
Between men and women
Thanks for reading, maybe relating
To my problems, motivations
My past and current situations

Dayvaughn Jerome Mays

2. THANKFUL

I'm still here
My life has shifted gears
From fifth to first
Blessed from cursed
Sitting in my own house instead of a hearse
From doing dirt, to getting dirty in my garden
From running the streets swerving, to legally serving
Burning hydro, and experiencing Shiloh
Love and respect everywhere I go
Because I give it to everybody, friend or foe
I don't pretend to know, I only grow, because I'm still hungry
I have to get knowledge and apply wisdom, that's real money
It feels funny talking about my past
Still wearing Dickies, but I try not to sag
I don't brag, I could lose it tomorrow
I could be on the corner talking about, can I borrow?
I'm still here, YHWH don't make mistakes
The things I've done must be ingredients in his cake
My life is a party given to me to ride like a Harley
Invite danger, but manage the challenge
Control my anger and conceal my talons
Reveal my talents and they can't believe like Jack Palance
Now I'm balanced like a squirrel from in my mothers stomach curled
I've come a long way and I love what's in my world

Dayvaughn Jerome Mays

3. THE SEARCH

In my world, I'm looking for my pearl
I'm kicking up sand in the mouth of the clam
Staying away from high demands
I want what's not expected
You don't usually see the most valuable things
Because they're protected
It's the unadorned that's ignored, and left neglected, disrespected
Perfection's not often reflected but, the best is what I seek
Not what's right for everyone, but for me
What you think is cute, I'd probably stay mute,
What you think is nice, I'd give different advice
What you charge for living large
I might lower the price
What you skim through once, I'm going over twice
I need to know what's right
My life depends upon the search
Not the ending
Because from the beginning
Ping pong back and forth with the court within my conscience
The wrong way is only deadly, when someone's in the path of nonsense

Dayvaughn Jerome Mays

4. HER

My face twisted up like I ate something sour
I knew right away I would have to use my powers
I'm about to drop more game than the twin towers
The hour is early, her teeth are pearly
A flower in the sun
I'm the bee who has come
To gather her pollen
Her fragrance is calling
No holograms, the real Dayvaughn
The Israelite who wants you as a blessing
The one I can't pass up no question
No Western philosophy could understand this possibly
No Eastern wise men could see the nirvana your eyes send
So, I spend 5 seconds to think this through
So, I recall my life's lessons and everything I think is true
No coincidences
This doesn't just happen
Some things are mysterious
Why aint I just mackin?
Simply asking her name was not enough
I wanted to know everything, but I also wanted her to hush
Please listen to my convictions about
How I don't know you but I think I figured you out
You were sent to alter the life I thought I lead
We need to go to the alter
Don't worry how this may seem
My dreams of pimpin and playing the field are dull
If I was married to the game, it has just been annulled

My skull has been hard and I've had to bump my head
Good judgment has been barred and made poor choices instead
With that said, you can right every wrong
From your inspiration, I can write every song
The breath to my lungs is supplied by the one who sent
You to be the turning point in a life spent
Living for the physical ignoring the mystical
Looking for science to explain the miracle
The spiritual person I need to be immersed in
Now it's your turn
This is where my verse ends

Dayvaughn Jerome Mays

5. MY LOVE

My love, she give's me my hugs
Her rubs are soft like a thick cotton cloth
Love it when we venture off and get lost
We always have a laugh, a glass of Patron
And just one lime
She likes it strong
Then we listen to her jazz songs
We could always be alone
We zone out on the couch or on the floor
I can always have more of my amore
The store's, they don't have what she can offer
I'm her number 1 shopper
When she gets to cracking jokes, I can't stop her
To top her, it would have to be her twin
From her mind to her grins
But I still might have to send for my love
From her look's to her taste I get buzzed
No matter what she does it's not enough
I'm a spoiled little kid no matter where she is
I will always have to live with my love

Dayvaughn Jerome Mays

6. 4:29

I received a different sunshine
That kind that doesn't blind
I can look in the eyes
Because it's not in the sky
I can enjoy without shades
I'll receive all her sunrays
Give all my concern
Help her grow up and learn
Sofia my daughter
You've made me a father
My guard has raised
My creator I praise
Oct 4th, you have come forth
I'm fulfilling the command
Be fruitful and multiply
Subdue the land
I'll teach what I can
Always hold your hand
The Torah will be your education
Your guide and medication
May my life be a demonstration
Of faith and endurance
Unconditional love and my best
That's my assurance
May YHWH do the rest
Shalom
Be blessed!

Dayvaughn Jerome Mays

7. MOVE

Sitting up to crawling
Pulling up on stuff to walking
Training wheels to a Schwinn
Rolling on stock to custom rims
How you get around I recommend
However you can
A bike, your feet, the bus, a van
Get sand in your shoes
Just stay on the move
Put on some aqua socks
If your feet are going to be wet
Get some awesome shocks
If you off-road or in the vet
Don't piss off the cops
If you haven't got a ticket yet
Take an R.V. see the country
Get pulled through snow by huskies
Make sure what you look for gets found
No matter what it takes to get around

Dayvaughn Jerome Mays

8. FAMILY

Man, women and child
Land, sea and the wild
The Creator must be proud
For making this up
I thank him for waking us up
My cup is full, I don't mind overflow
I'm a king, but don't rule over my bro
It's hard to know bad when you live good
A pretty lady and pretty baby, it's understood
The blessing is confirmation I should
Live up to potential and get after life credentials
Life is sweet as Winchell's, when you do the right thing
Bad things happen, just to let the light bring
The warmth and a reminder that there's a provider
Someone who brings together and a divider
That does for you, what you do for yours
Food shelter and more
Ignore him and you ignore them
Insure your family from their souls to their limbs
Keep your thoughts cleansed, don't think they don't get muddy
When it gets ugly you got a buddy
One who knows what a lie is and what's true
Involve him in your day to day; he's your family too

Dayvaughn Jerome Mays

9. COLORADO

I'm in the cloud city; we get summer days in winter
The present and the past cowboys and tech centers
Snow mobiles and Corvettes is how we can get around the set
Central City and Black Hawk will take your bets
Guest be warned or you can take the test
Please believe the truth that you heard aint stretched
Bring an extra lung we don't sale no breath
Email the world we gone tell the rest
Prepare the press, we smoke amongst the best
Blow exotic chronic and we sell the stress
We aint as high as the comets, but close to the crest
Three main freeways when we play
If you can find Colfax
Relax, you're o.k.
You thought it was just a ghost town with bars and banks
Let me boast about NORAD
Jets and tanks
Can you manage the Rapids in the Rockies and shake down a Nugget?
Ride a Bronco as it's bucking?
Live through an Avalanche and love it?
This is how we does it
Me, maw and paw
Don't get it twisted
I hope you are quick on the draw

Dayvaughn Jerome Mays

53

10. MY DAY

Grab my wallet and my Iphone
My bag full of pine cones then I head out the door
Hop in my Saturn and begin my pattern
On how I got to get more money more
Get a hold of contacts, negotiate contracts
Compensate myself a sweet price
Talking to investors, the unfair market molesters
I'm guilty, but my pockets feel nice
See there's a slight urgency for me to get currency before we head into Iran
I'm a little nervous of someone getting urges and be the next to drop
    the bomb
I aint tryna be the Don
Just smoke a little cron and put my feet up in my office
Converse with other bosses while me and my people floss
Throw some money at a particular thing hoping it's not a loss
I'll be in the sauna watching the piranha
How it turns out, I guess we'll see
Well its Obama, will he bring new pain and drama, they don't know
    what's best for me
A new daddy and a first mama to compliment Adam as they feed us
    from the tree
I'll be on the j.o.b.
Getting people high till 3:30 comes and I go free
Three 8 hour rotations
Sleep, work, and play station
Committing madden murder
Feeding the baby Gerber
Then I crash like a server

It could be easier
I could be a sheep herder
Walking with my staff watching over the calves
No worries sitting in the grass and just relax
The reality is the day is so fast
The night goes by and you wake up and wonder why
Should I make a check list, live wild and reckless?
How do I know all the facts aren't guesses?
Maybe it's best to play my part line by line
Close my eyes and protect my goal line

Dayvaughn Jerome Mays

11. THE JOB

Walking the shelves
Counting grams and ml's
Touching so many bottles like I'm reading braile
From a small team
To the take over by Walgreens
Senior Med
We get prescriptions read
Bring in meds and get it to the patients bed
Either UPS or on the Fed-x sled
If its local, it goes with a smaller courier instead
We get it done, c.s.r. pv1
Production, pv2
Into shipping
Boxed to you
Auto Med, LTC, Alf
Some days stressed
It don't matter
There's still laughter
Even in the face of disaster
10 pages 6 o'clock
New admits uh oh Dayvaughn, something's out of stock
Qs1 down
First doses
Irritated, but focused
What's a refill?
What must go?

Why so much now?
Today was slow, thank you
Fridays' a brief end
We will do it Monday all again

Dayvaughn Jerome Mays

12. THE OLD ROUTINE

Pull up to the Blue Bird
My cup's about 2/3
Smoking on some blue herb
This is how I do dirt
The crowds excited because I got some new turds
About to spit a few words
You gotta hear my new verse
So sick, get you a nurse
Better yet pick a hearse
I'm killin' em but, it's a slow curse
No witch doctor
No séance
No church
Can get me out since I've been in the game's purse
Like my man Q, it's about time I burse,
The people rang for me
You can call me Lurch
First things first
F.A.M.I.L.E I am We
Since 91 B2B
Real men want what lions need
Females who chose me to breed project my name
Spread my seed and floss my mane
Show my teeth and protect my team
Kill to eat, even if that means you
I don't steal, that's weak
That's what thieves do
We move paper from pockets to accounts

We move populations while you move an ounce
Too late
School is out
Meeting is adjourned
Get off the stage
It's my turn

Dayvaughn Jerome Mays

13. NEW ROUTINE {the inner lotto}

Barley broke and success hungry with a team like Tony Dungy
Time to rise like the sun and get money
Applications didn't reply
Now on my mouthpiece, I will rely
I see my ribbon in the sky, but it aint for love
But thanks to the Most High above
Hugs and kisses
Pictures and autographs
Now I can go and get things I don't have
New house, new car
New shoes, new me
New rules
New job to do with few tools
Pens, pads, laptops and keyboards
To the uncreative, I can be your
Greeting card writer or ad seller
Radio jingle or movie trailer
I can thank my tailor for me looking so sharp
But I must thank my Creator for giving me insight on the art
Of story telling and composing words like Mozart
Dark thoughts become illuminated
The heart stops in between beats
What's in between the transfer for those seconds do we cheat?
I want to meet truly happy and end the pursuit
To most that don't compute
Like having a dispute with a mute
Is it possible to get your joy to stand still?
Recognize your blessing and make it your obsession and you will

Dayvaughn Jerome Mays

14. IT BEGINS

Things ain't the same when I ride through
My city is getting bigger
My eyes frame and capture the picture
I filter out doubts about what I need to do to make it
Where I come from enables
Me to beat the house and win the table
Better yet brake it
I'm stable now, but I can improve
Maybe it'll take something that puts me on the news
Not by braking the rules
How about an invention?
I won't re-invent the wheel
Just talk about what I feel
Drill, baby drill
Tap the oil in my minds soil
I'm coiled and ready to strike
Absorbing life I'm ready to write
All my wrongs I'm ready to right
All along my career has been postponed
Now I have my mojo
My journey begins like Frodo

Dayvaughn Jerome Mays

15. THE MAIN EVENT

Pick up the phone or log on to the band wagon
Let money be the reason that your pants are saggin
Having the power to negotiate
Pulling out of your pocket what you can appropriate
Create the demand for a superior brand
Available at all locations
Something the people want at home or on vacation
In this nation of grind you want to have
Never asking what happened to mine
This is your time, it's the main event
Money gets made to get spent, that's the intent
This information should be in print, before you give a cent
Know the laws
This is a marathon, not a sprint
Sick of barely making rent?
Tired of working for the temps?
Getting fired for putting fire to the hemp
Are you content?
Or does the system have your consent?
The only way out is spit
Get anti-employee
Commit to the main event
Edit the script and change your story
Business and pleasure mix
Taking trips, writing it off on your taxes
Travel the world axis to axis

Dayvaughn Jerome Mays

16. WHO'S A POET?

Who's a poet, who's a pro at what they do like this?
I'm not well known, but on my own
I use my pen to kiss
Wine and dine each and every line
My rhyme is paced
Embrace this paper like a loved one and feel my grace
If ears could taste, they would lust for my plush rhymes
I like to steal the show, so I go to the back of lines
A thin line between good and bad
Can't you tell?
Innovated and elevated like Colorado's Vail.
Smell the essence of this written present that I share
I stare into your eyes with my words with the privilege
Of knowing that I'm sowing seeds seen in the poet's village
A fin-less fish has dove into your wishing well and now dwells
In your imagination, the poet who glows with lyrical collaboration
The situations good like it should be
Sweating for expressions
I don't want to cease
I've held back so long I've over spilled
I must yield and build a dam
So I can preserve my skill

Dayvaughn Jerome Mays

17. THE HEADACHE

I'm suffering
I need bufferin for my headache
Staring at the red and blue states
Is it too late to save the empire?
Can't trust the info, if you inquire
We need Richard Pryor back
So he can make a liar
Out of the so-called facts
Why we attacked the wrong countries
Over tax the hungry
Demand real talk from dummies
At least they don't claim the rocky road ain't bumpy
Wonder why the people grumpy
The pump keeps money flowing
But the economy is slowing
The deficit is growing too high
You can't count it
The horse is too big, you can't mount it
Why we looking astounded
Since the country has been founded
We have seen corruption and seduction
Consumption of freedoms
The world used to look to us as a beacon

Dayvaughn Jerome Mays

18. TOMORROW AINT PROMISED

Live it up because tomorrow aint promised
Be honest
Don't ignore those who genuinely admonish
Why live committing nonsense
You can enjoy life
Without employing dice
Taking chances that's not worth it
As long as there's a purpose
Take some time to research it
Tomorrow aint promised doesn't mean be stupid
Do what makes you happy be careful around cupid
Get money, but don't get caught
If it doesn't feel right, go with your first thought
Stop and smell the flowers
Use your powers
Get out the hood and see the outskirts
The world is ours
The world is to be explored and not trampled
To be inspected, but not dismantled
Be the example as you scramble
We might look at you and see you on the discovery channel

Dayvaughn Jerome Mays

19. CROSSROADS

I'm staring at the crossroads
The daring place of lost souls
The race ends in last place
A winner is not known
Life's loan rates are higher and there's no fires
Just ice cold
There are things I need to off-load
To get there, I had to off-road
I'm a dropped stone
Sinking fast in a vast zone
A sad song where all the instruments have a bad tone
I need some backbone and faith to get me back home
The track's gone
I'll look at the stars
I have no car and I lack a phone
In fact, this poem is guiding me to my moment in time
Where I'll get back to the straight and narrow
With my crossroads behind
No longer blinding and binding linking me to the crimes
Against the covenant, I miss loving it
It wasn't me
Just a lie

Dayvaughn Jerome Mays

20. THE WRONG HERO

Hidden in my waist is something to be embraced
People aint safe better stay out my way
A stray bullet may strike
Watch the fight if you like
Throw blows or I can throw slugs that make doughnut holes
My clothes barely fit, but I don't trip
I'm a gangster, I don't keep feelings
I keep danger
Don't arose my anger
I got more tools than Granger
Bats and crow bars
You'll show scars and bruises
You'll see stars, but they don't make music
Black and blue busted lips you must have pissed
Somebody off good in the hood or close to it
Almost made a ghost at an early age stupid
Sitting in a dirty grave being remembered on a page
Don't walk on the stage if you aint ready for action
No cut from the director
Better have that protector
No matter what sector
Your home or out of bounds
I'll make mummies out of clowns and drown the weak fish
I'm a killer whale that's an opportunist
I won't make a sound when I rob you like Lummis
If you aint ready for this lifestyle, I urge you not to do this
Scarface said gangsters don't live that long, it's foolish
Don't be an investigator without this tip and clueless

Dayvaughn Jerome Mays

21. THE BLUES

I never liked the blues until I realized it was the news
The truth and the untrue events watched over coffee and cigarettes
Or murr and frankincense
So intense and so entrenched are some stories
Others don't make sense, some bore me
Some facts, some hints, some statements, most arguments
What are you for? What are you against?
Now I choose the blues
The mystery is unraveled
I had the clues I just didn't know it
Didn't know the rules, the lifeless but priceless jewels
One's not found in stores and rarely found in schools
Whose blues are more blue? Whose blues are you?
Whose blues are due? Whose blues get unblued?

Dayvaughn Jerome Mays

22. WHAT YOU GONNA DO FOR ME?

Haven't you done enough?
I pay the high taxes, live among the masses
Avoiding car crashes
Dodging cigarette ashes
Maybe I need glasses?
I don't see you do enough besides a talk over lunch
I see your lips moving, but is it just a bluff?
I hear a whole lot of ruff, but wit no bite
Gas so high, I need to ride to work on my bike
Get you some Timberlands and maybe take a hike
Give me my Constitution; I'm sick of the intrusion
All the new institutions, all the illusions, the delusions
Confusion, the using and misusing, it aint amusing
Driving folks to boozing and losing hope
Losing jobs, losing houses, losing spouses
Today the doubts are so high they sky scrape
And I'm only talking about my state

Dayvaughn Jerome Mays

23. BAIL OUT

Can I get some help?
I need my house paid off
Can I get some help?
I just got laid off
Can I get a tax break?
Had to fire my supplier
He sold me a bag of shake
Said it would get me higher
Can I get some help?
Can you fill my tank?
By the way, do I need to be a bank?
I need a blank check
So I can build me a deck
Can I get some help?
Instead planning another war
How about drilling off shore?
Like gulf island where there's more
Enough for years and years
Stop the flow of blood and tears
You don't want to help
Unless you can take over
You want nothing else
Than for more control
Until you smother
I can help myself
It might be harder
I might struggle
Long as you don't take away
My overtime and my side hustle

Dayvaughn Jerome Mays

24. CAN YOU SEE IT?

What's coming over the airwaves is conformation
Of unfair days, a glared glaze, you can't see what's in your face?
Try to keep pace in a race with nitro vs. 2 legs
The losers drink a few kegs and stare over a ledge
I don't pledge allegiance; I'm filing a grievance for indecent proposals
Bicoastal politics, keeping the country sick
Worried about Michael Vick instead focusing on the oil slick
Companies with whom they keep company with
Isn't it something, we keep voting and hoping for the best?
Take this pill for stress
Take this one for pain
This one here will help you refrain from using your brain
Let the government lead, from the cradle to the grave
Be a good citizen, tell on those menacing, but ignore the missing dividends
The Pentagon reports, the media distorts, as long as we can watch sports
And still smoke on our porch, we will put up with the forced doctrines
One sided arguments
Monkeys turned to men
If I sit in the water long enough, will I grow a fin?
Or in the dirt, am I certain to grow a stem?
Design has a designer, ignitions have an igniter
I don't believe in an atheist for one reason
You say there's no one out there because you didn't see him?
Can you see atoms? Can you see your liver?
You didn't see the mail man, but the mail got delivered
No Torah, no Quran, look in a mirror
If there is life, there must be a life giver!

Dayvaughn Jerome Mays

25. AROUND THE CORNER

Revolution in the distance
The penalty is the death sentence
Unless you claim repentance
Lose your backbone, go back home
It will be televised, tell your eyes it's a lie
This isn't marshal law
Those aren't tanks in the streets
We don't have a curfew
Why haven't I eaten in a week?
Cause I'm weak and don't except it
Rather conform, than correct it
The government is reckless
No matter who's elected
The checks and balances
Really don't amount to spit
Let's roll up an ounce of spliffs
And listen to Malcolm spit
Better recite the Torah quick
Before they get to burning books
All the prosecutors
Are about to turn to crooks
Hand outs and soup lines
Former rich men doing shoe shines
Senators are sinister
Mischievous ministers
Watch the cook, he's fixing to stir
The American boiling pot
Is hot and ready

The regal eagle is no more flying steady
You hardly see a Chevy
Everything is imported
Our education is failing
Our entertainment is snorted
To ignore is to support it
I'm guilty as a watcher
Kicking it like a game of soccer
Misdiagnosing like a doctor
Malpractice
Will the next President be an actress?
This is what I think about while laying on my mattress

Dayvaughn Jerome Mays

26. OPTIMISTIC

It Looks like they Baracked the vote
Now lets see if he will rock the boat
Lots of hope in the first colored man
They want to see if they can
Stretch his rubber band
Other than a moment in history
Is it a part of the prophecy?
The mystery?
How will he be remembered in a century?
Will his presidency be a ministry?
Will he be compatible with the powers that be?
Will there be a disconnect or a cohesive chemistry?
Continued economic misery or produce a surplus?
I know you're nervous
Will he serve us or be another puppet for the rich, a bitch for Buffet?
Fill our bucket or cut a whole in the empty one?
Is he taking a shot with an empty gun?
The slums to the gate guarded
The loving to the hate hearted
We'll be all eyes
Will he be a champion or a fall guy?
Tall lies and small truths?
Will he fall victim to another Wilkes Booth?
A spoof or proof that culture is critical to run a country to the ground
Or take it to the pinnacle?

Dayvaughn Jerome Mays

27. UNCOMMON QUESTIONS

Do grass blades make lawns?
Do rain drops make oceans?
Did pleasure and pain make the Psalms?
Is poison a potion?
Is death an emotion that's mistakenly chosen?
Or just a heart that's broken?
If words could not be spoken would our eyes pass judgement?
How would you know when someone's joking?
How could you open up and express?
Would we touch to impress and wait for consequence?
Would smiles themselves except the compliment?
Reflect accomplishment?
Are we hard wired for interaction?
Is our scent a calling?
An unspoken attraction?

Dayvaughn Jerome Mays

28. TONGUES

Foreign tongues sound good like foreign drums
They make you wonder what they say
What is that note that they play?
It separates
Remember when we tried to elevate and build the tower of Babel
But it was stopped at Heavens gate
The great debate is what's the original
Hebrew? Aramaic? What else is admissible?
Yubal played the first harp and flute
Until language, were we just mute?
Acappella were the songs
Until music came along
Who made the first alphabet?
Who played in the first band?
Who was the first fan?
Now English is the international language
Because we are the super power
But will we lose and be confused if we build another tower?

Dayvaughn Jerome Mays

29. THE BIRDS AND THE BEES

There's more than birds
There's words in the breeze
There's curves in the leaves
Waves of water move seas
Its hot now, then the ease
Giant giraffes to the fleas
What trees breathe out, we breathe
So pleased to see a sunset, will it cease? Not one yet
The excitement mixed with mystery
The universe
The history
Why whisper? Who's listening?
Is it trespassing or visiting?
Are we that hungry?
Why the overfishing?
Insisting we must explore what's up and not among us
Have we already outgrown our compass?
Have we found and named all the fungus?
Don't let the oceans depth numb us
So much to see
So many flowers for the bees
Rain showers bring a piece of the elements
It may drown what creeps
But for the elephant, relief from the heat on the African plains
Those in China to Australia all the same
So strange but true, the place we live gives a blue sky
Then a new light at night so far away, but not out of sight

Planted just right in the heights
It delights my eyes to see this amazing consistent but ever-changing
     world made for me
The birds and the bees

Dayvaughn Jerome Mays

30. SCRIPTURE IS LIQUOR

It can be bitter and be sweet
Not bias for the strong and the weak
For the aggressive and the meek
Moses to Malachi
Today the same rules apply
The wisdom of Solomon
The brave king David
Blessings to those who love it
Corrections to those who hate
Just myths and legends?
12's and 7's?
Witches and giants
Riches and defiance
Lions and dragons
Silence and bragging
The Nile to the Euphrates
Boring stories to the amazing
Fact or fiction
Class or prison
Lessons learned
Impressions burned
Proverbs absorbed
Directions turned
Rising concerns on truths within
Or just an idea introduced to men?

Dayvaughn Jerome Mays

31. WHOSE RULES?

All sounds don't come from music
I think gun shots are acoustic
We make the rules slick, so they don't stick
There's loop holes in everything, but don't trip
This is a poem also a story told in rhyme
I give a line to make you have a thought; now rewind
Did he write what I was thinking?
He was looking; I was blinking
Linking everyday to the past, it's the last word
That's usually remembered and delivered as the fast curve
Pay attention when they mention backwards
Democracy and freedom, what do they mean? Go and read them
If the majority is wrong then the song is sung in error
One man's freedom fighter is another man's terror
Better to live alone than in a home of hate
No need to escape if you provide your own plate
Can we all get along as if we need to?
The global citizen is what they feed you
But whose rules will prevail?
The dictator?
The Prime Minister?
The male?
Is it for sale to the highest bidder?
Beginners follow or become the leaders of tomorrow?
Is religion the winner?
The pious or the sinner?
The illuminated or the dimmer?
Who will render judgements? Do the sinless cast the first stone?

Put everybody under one umbrella is the first wrong
No bongs but, you can have a cigarette
You can drink; have you destroyed your liver yet?
American discrimination is invitation to confusion
Is it the land of the free or just a song that we are using?
For amusing purposes, can you answer whose Earth this is?
This is where it gets shaky like nervousness
Give everyone an acre
Do everyone a favor
Give them self employment as their governor or their mayor
Out source jobs of the tailor, butcher, and baker
Thought to hand; then to pen to paper
I wonder how many besides me will read this later
This flavor is a compound; the recipe is teachable, calm down
Without anyone around who are you going to con now?

Dayvaughn Jerome Mays

32. HAVE YOU EVER?

Have you ever wanted to express yourself?
To tell a story or address your health?
Mentally or physical?
Talk about the every day or the mystical
Find a common thread to build?
Most people share a common field
Sometimes we vent to heal
Or just simply share how we feel
I deal with my actions and distractions
By writing for the world and looking for reaction
Was I on point or dead wrong on that one?
Coming from the heart; the seat of passion
Unmasking the person you see
We may have talked before, but do you know me?
If you like, may you find the time
To pick apart, chew, spew or digest each line?

Dayvaughn Jerome Mays